Dearest

CW00428515

Timeless Love

Life is full of
Supruses,

Prepare To Be Surprised

By Jennifer M Maddy

Lots of Love &

Blessings   Jen xxxx

Timeless Love

This book was first published in Great Britain in paperback during March 2019.

The moral right of Jennifer M Maddy is to be identified as the author of this work and has been asserted by her in accordance with the Copyright, Designs and Patents Act of 1988.

All rights are reserved and no part of this book may be produced or utilized in any format, or by any means, electronic or mechanical, including photocopying, recording or by any information storage or retrieval system, without prior permission in writing from the publishers - Coast & Country/Ads2life.
Email: ads2life@btinternet.com

All rights reserved.

ISBN-13: 9781090332004

Copyright © March 2019 Jennifer M Maddy

CONTENTS

Page

About the Author

Jennifer Maddy is a Qualified Reiki Grand Master, IET (Integrated Energy Therapy) Master, Practitioner & Teacher.

She is also qualified as a Psychic Surgeon. Her Gift as a Light Worker is to "Share her Love & Light" and guide and mentor Souls to connect to the Divine Wisdom WITHIN on their Spiritual Journey to Enlightenment.

Jennifer currently has her own Holistic Spiritual Practice.

She lives in Barleyfield Kilcurry, Dundalk, Co Louth. Ireland.

Jennifer currently works as an Inclusion Classroom Assistant in St. Louis Secondary School, Dundalk.

ACKNOWLEDGEMENTS

I wish to express my sincere and heartfelt appreciation to the following.

Teresa Maddy, my INSPIRATION, mum, friend and mentor.

Ben & Leanne Sullivan. My children and the joy my Life. A sincere thankyou to my daughter for co-writing my story with me and for having such patience and understanding. My son Ben for putting up with the two of us , So proud of both of you.

Don. Hale OBE and Dr Steve Green for their contributions.

Lorraine Quigley, my Soul friend and mentor. Thankyou for taking the TIME to preview and correct book and for all your Wisdom and Guidance through our Lifetime.

Brenda Woods Finegan, for creating the Writespace for creative Writing. For opening my mind to new ideas and possibilities.

Most of all, thank you Spirit, for the most wonderful, amazing, magical gift of life. Thankyou Spirit for the special gift of my Guardian Angel, and all the other angels, spirit guides, family and friends who continue to protect and guide me from the celestial realms, showering me with so many heavenly blessings and abundance.

Thankyou to my family, extended Soul Family & Soul Family Cluster Worldwide. I am one of a larger Network & communion of Souls united and extending our Love throughout the Planet raising our own Spiritual Consciousness and the Spiritual Consciousness of All Mankind.

Reviews

A Spiritual gem! A beautiful book, where Jennifer Maddy speaks from the heart.

We all come to this earth energy vibration frequency to learn lessons, in order to progress on our Spiritual path, to raise our own Spiritual awareness and the collective Spiritual consciousness of all humanity.

Jennifer, through relating her own painful experiences of facing cancer and a marriage break-up, teaches us in a loving and compassionate way, how we need to look at everything that happens to us and everyone who comes into our lives as having a purpose. Jennifer pushes us even further and teaches us how to be grateful for all negative experiences, because it is in dealing with these that we enable our soul to expand. And life is all about soul expansion!

Beautifully written and with humour, Jennifer's amazing energy just oozes out from every page! You will not be able to put this book down! A wonderful addition to Spiritual literature!

Eileen McCourt- Reiki Grand Master,
Spiritual author and teacher.

"Timeless Love captures the essence of loving in every area of a person's life. How Happiness, Sadness, Joy Tears, Laughter and Forgiveness can conquer everything in life. Jennifer writes from her heart, which is illustrated in this Spellbinding Book. Jennifer displays her Life Journey, Highs and Lows through her Truth. Jennifer is a True Inspiration and a Spiritual Master and Mentor for both Young and Old. A Divine Channel of Love and Light."

Dymphna Turley, Life Coach, Faith Angelz.

In her beautifully written book, Jennifer Maddy openly and lovingly takes us through her awakening, her jolt out of herself and her soul's journey back to full recognition of its purpose and connection to all that is, the very essence of her being. We would all do well to read it taking at least one eye off our own narrow minded vision of our lives in this earthly realm and centring it on the flame that burns within, as Jennifer puts it, the I AM force that can only lead us to our higher calling. A story of love, loss searching and unity that has shaped the authors life in unimaginable ways!

Lorraine Quigley

The Right Space

Close your eyes.
Take 3 deep breaths. Breathe in slowly and exhale.
Well done.
Feel your body begin to relax. Let the tension ease from
your shoulders.
You are SAFE, in a sacred space.
You are so LOVED.
Feel your own energy....
How are you feeling? Do you feel pain in any particular
area? What does it feel like?
If you could taste, touch smell or express the feeling in
colour, words or vision, what would you say?

Jennifer:

I feel LOST.

Therapist:

Well done. Now let's drop in a little deeper....... What do
you see, feel, taste or smell?

Jennifer:

I see a little baby girl hovering in the air, unattached,
floating in endless time and space. She is feeling innocent
and vulnerable. She does not know where she is going.
SHE IS ME!

LITTLE SOUL & THE SUN

by Neale Donald Walsch.

Little Soul gets ready for Life on Earth. God reminds her that she is the Light and nothing but the Light. God tells the little Soul that while on earth, she gets to express herself as part of the Light she wants to be....

LOVE, PEACE, JOY, POWER etc....

Whatever she wishes.

The little Soul eventually chooses to be FORGIVING, which God warns her comes with some danger. The little Soul willing to take the chance, promises she will forgive any hurts from people, places and situations in this lifetime. God informs the little Soul that it is possible she might forget who she really is for a long time as she experiences Life and its lessons. She had a choice to choose Light or Darkness!

So what particular aspect or aspects of Light and Love, True Essence and Presence are you here to express. Perhaps each of us did indeed decide before we were born, the particular gifts, parts of Love and Light we were here to express and it's simply a matter of taking the time to Go WITHIN to remember.

Please enjoy my life story as I share my love with you and let it   trigger emotions or stored memories locked in your subconscious.
ENJOY.

Chapter One
Where it began...

Born on the 7th August 1970, my life began with a bang! Unlike the stereotypical new baby celebration encompassed by love, joy and happiness, my journey into the world was surrounded by fear, loneliness and secrecy. My birth mother fell pregnant with me outside of wedlock. Although in our modern society this is widely accepted, during the 1970's it was an extremely taboo situation and was widely judged and unaccepted, especially in catholic homes. Due to this, my birth mother spent the last few months of her pregnancy alone in Castlepollard mother and baby home in county Meath hiding her pregnancy. Her journey to this temporary abode, miles away from any family or friends, is a real indicator of her fear of judgment and a desperate attempt to hide this forbidden pregnancy from the rest of the world. Without any surprise, given the situation, she decided to put me up for adoption. When all the paperwork was signed and sealed, and at only a few weeks old, I was delivered to my new family and my birth mother returned home as though nothing had ever happened.

As for me, I was adopted into the Maddy family. I was blessed with a loving home in Barleyfield, Kilcurry, a small yellow bungalow surrounded by an abundance of green fields, ever-green trees and an endless number of multi-colored begonias. This place became my kingdom, my safe place, my forever home, my utopia. My Father Denis (now deceased) adored the ground I walked on. From the first moment that he held me in his arms, I became his little princess. He would walk the streets of Dundalk showing me off to the world. I became his pride and joy, his baby girl, his perfect little bundle of love. However, it didn't continue to flow just as smoothly as it had begun. Just as all our life paths tend to twist and turn, my new path had some lumps and bumps along the way too. Shortly after I was adopted, my adopted mum Teresa found out that she was pregnant with a baby boy. The excitement and joy associated with the news of a new baby was soon overshadowed by fear. When the social workers realised that one form had not been signed by my birth mother, the act of finalising my adoption hung by a thread. They sent letter after letter to the given address in England, each of which was returned labelled "RETURN TO SENDER". My new mum was terrified! She was afraid to tell anyone about her wonderful news in case it would have a detrimental impact on my adoption. She had to hide her pregnancy for months on end, even to the extreme of lying about her due date, all in order to ensure that I remained theirs. She couldn't bear the thought of losing me. Not now! Not after all the love and affection that had been shared between us. She refused to be separated from me. I was her daughter! Thankfully this nightmare never became a reality. The adoption agency finally found blood relations in Ireland. They traced me back to my mother's parents living in Kerry and told them that a baby girl had been given up for adoption by their daughter. What a terrible way for my birth family to find out about my existence. Eventually, the forms where signed and Mr and Mrs Maddy received full custody of me. I was now their daughter, a secure part of their family. I was now Jennifer Maddy. And how lucky was I!

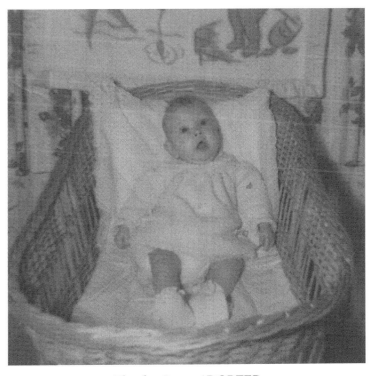

The day I was ADOPTED

My baby brother Andrew was born 9 months and 3 days later, on the 10th May 1971. We were what they call "Irish Twins", with less than a year between us. Our family unit was now complete. I was exactly where I was supposed to be at the right time, in the right place and with the right family. I had a very happy childhood and I was loved unconditionally. I believed I was very special because I was adopted. My parents told me this from a very early age and I accepted this as normal and never questioned it. The love, care and encouragement I received from my family was all I needed. I vaguely remember a beautiful summer's day, sitting on a tiny wooden seat in my former primary school, in Kilcurry, Co Louth. The teacher was chatting about family and how everyone has 2 mums, their mum and Our Lady. My brother Andrew who was and still is a cheeky devil, put his hand up and in all his innocence blurted out "Our Jennifer is special. She has 3 mums". I felt a warm glow fill my heart as the realisation that this statement was true triggered a feeling of excitement within me. I didn't quite know what it meant but it sounded good! I was special. I was happy to be me.

Sitting in my garden in Barleyfield, Kilcurry, Dundalk

Reminiscing on my childhood, I am filled with many happy memories. I remember as if it were yesterday, my summer holidays in Gyles' Quay, just north of Dundalk. The summers back in the 70s seemed to be always hot. We would pack up a picnic every Sunday and head to the beach. How I looked forward to Sundays all week. We would park at the pier and meet up with our friends. However, not all of these memories are filled with sunshine and happiness. One memory that I can picture as clear as day is my little red swimsuit. I always thought I was overweight and as a result, I would hide in the car until no one was looking and then sprint as fast as my legs would allow until I reached the pier edge. I would throw myself off the pier and dive into the water. Only then, could I relax and enjoy the moment. When I look back on pictures, I realise I was not overweight at all. I had a lovely figure, even in my little red swimsuit. If only I had realised at the time, at that young age, how beautiful I was from the inside out. Learning how to open our eyes to our own inner beauty is a skill we could use to make the world a better place and create an easier journey for ourselves. My dad noticed how I felt about my appearance and encouraged me to join a Cross Country Running Club in Mountpleasant near my home. This was the best step forward for me as, not only did I get fit, but I developed social skills through interacting with all the girls and boys of my own age. I became part of a team for the first time. This was hard work and required discipline and dedication, but it was so rewarding and fun. I was not a fast runner but I had stamina. I loved running. I loved the freedom it gave me as I felt the wind in my hair and the air on my face.

Fresh air. Freshness. Freedom.

Mountpleasant Running Club also held discos to fundraise for the club. These turned into the highlight of my social life. I loved to dance. I would spend nights on end twisting and twirling all over the dancefloor. My dad, being dad, helped supervise at these discos. He would tell me it was asked of him as he was a member of the club. However, I suspected it was to keep an eye on me and to ensure I was always ok. His love for me was radiant. It encompassed our entire relationship. I felt so safe, so loved and I had so much fun.

Chapter Two
Saying YES

As secondary school days approached, my security blanket, my comfort zone and that feeling of timeless safety began to slightly fade. I was a bit overwhelmed by secondary school. The crowds of green uniformed figures marching in the long, high-ceilinged corridors, the hustle and bustle in the locker rooms and the ever-changing faces from class to class were all unfamiliar to me. I felt as though I blended in with the walls, just one of many, not so special anymore. However this was ok with me. I didn't want to be noticed or stand out. I was so shy. I felt out of my comfort zone in my huge green uniform. I was so disorganised. My schoolbag was always a mess, although in my head I knew where everything was. Amidst all of the chaos, I managed to get through my school years alive! Hurray! By the time I was a sixth year student, at the top of the school hierarchy, I was at ease. I had finally found my place there. At this stage, I loved school. I enjoyed every minute of it. The friends I made, the games we played, the journeys I encountered, I loved it all!

Today I am proud to say I work in my former Secondary School, St Louis, Dundalk as an SNA (Special Needs Assistant). I have always felt drawn to supporting children and helping them feel safe and loved. The ethos of the school and the SNA programme in general is to value ourselves and each child in our care. This role is extremely rewarding and I feel like I can encourage children to be proud of themselves and to grow to be confident young adults each in their own right, knowing that they are safe to express themselves freely. Each child is unique in their own individuality and each child has a role to fulfill in this world. We learn from each other. The title of my role has recently been changed from Special Needs Assistant to Classroom Inclusion Assistant and I believe that inclusion is much needed in our modern world. We must continue to strive for all to be included in our society and for our diversity, uniqueness and oneness to be recognised and embraced. I believe that I am here to remind people, both young and old, of the gifts that they have come here to express. I have learned that as each one of us discovers and steps into our true essence and the amazing gifts that come with it, we are activating and coming into alignment with our truth. Thankfully, mindfulness is becoming prominent on the syllabus of our Education System, which is very much needed. We are now supporting the children in our care by using a more holistic approach and nourishing their Mind, Body and Soul. Children thrive in this environment, as sometimes school is their only safe space due to circumstances outside of their control. I feel humbled to be part of this safe space, this amazing team and to be trusted with such an important role. I am here to make people feel special, and more importantly, feel proud to be special.

On reflection, I always fell into LUCK. I did not see this at the time. However looking back has given me a clearer, more grateful view of how my life has panned out. After I left school, I started working with the Permanent TSB Bank. At my very first interview I was told that I had the job. I stayed in the bank for 13 years. I am known as Jenny from the Bank. It was during this time that I made life-long friends, gained a lot of life experience and came to the conclusion that my calling in life was to help people. I wasn't sure at this point who or how I would help, but I knew that that's what I needed to do. We were the Bank that liked to say **YES**. Although this concept has recently changed, it has had a personal effect on me. It taught me to say yes. To say yes to *LIFE* To say yes to *LOVE*. To say yes to *HAPPINESS*.

In my mid-20s, I met my future husband. It all began in The Gym, a fitness centre in Dundalk. I loved the Gym and visited daily on my way home from work. It allowed me to relax after a busy day, while providing me with time to think, reflect and plan for the future, or manifest as I refer to it now. Benny was the gym instructor. I would spend my time telling him all my stories, everything that happened throughout the day and all my plans for the future. We became good friends. He knew me better than I knew myself. We discovered that we had a lot in common, we wanted the same things, we had the same outlook on life and we both wanted more than anything to enjoy life and to be happy. Our first date consisted of a four mile jog. I wish I could still do that now! We became good friends. We were young, innocent and in love. Benny owned a motorbike. We travelled around Ireland exploring the beautiful landscapes, the small country villages and the high-rise city towers. Life was so fast, carefree and fun. I would hold on to him so tightly, however as I was never afraid that I would fall off. I felt that sense of timeless safety again, like I was in a bubble of protection, like I had my very own bodyguard, my knight in shining armour. Before long, he proposed and no surprise, I said YES! We drove to Dublin in his little, brown car together and bought my ring. I was over the moon! I had never been so excited and the first thing I wanted to do was to tell my parents. I wanted to share this newfound happiness, this feeling of love, hope and joy and my overwhelming excitement with them more than anything.

Chapter Three
The ultimate heart break

The day I got engaged, I didn't tell my dad as I wanted all the family to be together when I shared my news. I remember kissing him good bye when I was going to bed that night, while he sat in his old armchair, the same chair upon which he had cuddled me and Andrew during our childhood. I contemplated spilling my exciting secret, but just as I was about to blurt it out, he asked me for one more kiss, a precious moment that I will always hold dear in my memory. The following evening, my brother Andrew and I came home on the bus and stopped at the Gym. As I walked through the door, I glanced at my father on the running machine. I waved hello and continued into the little office to see Benny. Suddenly, the other gym instructor came running into the office and told me to stay where I was, not to leave the little room. My brother had gone to talk to my dad as we entered the Gym. In mid conversation, my dad suddenly collapsed having suffered a massive heart attack. He fell to the ground. An ambulance was called and he was carried out and rushed to the Louth County Hospital in Dundalk. I was asked to get my mum. Benny and I drove to pick her up and rushed to the hospital. As we entered through the hospital doors, an eerie, horrible feeling fell over me. We were met by the doctor who told us that my dad had passed away. He had died in my brother's arms on the way to hospital. I didn't believe it. My dad; gone? He couldn't be! One minute I was so excited and happy about life and the next minute every ounce of life was taken from me, through the loss of a loved one. My father died on the 5th April 1993. His soul song is "Danny Boy." Each & every one of us has a soul song to sing. I thank you Denis Maddy for choosing to be my dad.

Adopted Soul Maddy Family. Denis, Teresa, Jennifer & Andrew

Thankfully, he did get an opportunity to see my engagement ring. The night before he died, when I was out with friends, my mum had secretly shown him the ring, which as yet, I was not wearing as we had not officially announced our 'news'. My dad was a watch mender by trade and he knew a lot about jewellery. He had taken out his magnifying glass and had inspected the ring. He was impressed and had approved of my marriage. I didn't really grieve my dad's death. I didn't give myself time to think about it. Instead, I threw myself into preparation. We began to plan for my wedding the following year.

I BURIED my EMOTIONS.

*This was the start of a repetitive process of not expressing how I felt. The main problem was that **I DIDNT KNOW HOW TO**!!!!!*

Chapter Four
My castle in the clouds

I was 24 when I got married. We were both young and innocent with no worries, just a whole lot of love and dreams. We just went with the FLOW. We never worried about trivial things such as money, or even where it would come from. However, it always appeared. As I already said, I was always in luck! We were manifesting so quickly, although we were not consciously aware of the POWER of our THOUGHTS.

"Will you Love, Honour & Obey me for the rest of your Life in Sickness & in Health, all the Days of my Life."

WORDS...

WHAT IS LOVE?

HOW DO YOU KNOW YOU'RE IN LOVE?

DO YOU LOVE YOURSELF?

DO YOU KNOW WHO YOU ARE?

DO YOU KNOW WHY YOU ARE HERE?

WHAT IS YOUR VOCATION?

Words have such energy & meaning. However, we didn't fully understand the meaning of these words with all the excitement, laughter and fun. As luck would have it, we bought a site from a dear friend Henry Dooley from 'The Hip'. We planned our dream house and worked towards making our dreams come true. We built a mansion in the clouds up in Faughart on the outskirts of Dundalk, right beside St Brigid's Shrine, a beautiful home on the side of a mountain with a magnificent view of the trees, the sea and the countryside. We moved into our home and slowly decorated every room as we dreamt it would be. What a very happy time in my life. I was living the dream. Just when I thought it couldn't get any better, it did! The following year I found out that I was pregnant, with would you believe, TWINS! Two for the price of one! What a coincidence right? My own readymade family! On the 6th February 1998, I gave birth to two bundles of JOY, Leanne and Ben, weighing in at 5lbs 5ozs and 5lbs 7ozs respectively. I was so blessed; my very own gifts from God. I finally felt how my mother and father had felt when they signed the final adoption papers, that overwhelming sense of unconditional love. I settled into motherhood with ease and I loved every minute of it. I still do! I remember walking the roads of Faughart with my old fashioned double buggy. I loved the peace and quiet and the tranquil countryside with its endless fields and a gorgeous forest to explore. I would regularly call to neighbours for tea and sit and chat as the children played happily outside. I often stopped off at

Faughart Shrine while out walking on my own and would sit there in silence, listening to the birds singing and feeling the warmth of the sun on my face breaking through the trees. The holy water there is blessed and I would drink the cold water flowing from the well. I prayed deeply and had great faith. I also remember Christmas times when Henry, the old man from the mountain, and I would go into the fields and pick fresh holly. He would tell me stories and poems of the history of Faughart. We often got a lot of snow fall and the children would be off school as our house was in a very remote location. They loved sliding and rolling down the hillsides and making snowmen. They would run through the fields during the summer and carve their names on trees. This time in my life was so precious and priceless and fills my heart with a warm glow now as I fondly think about it. The children in our care grow up so quickly in the blink of an eye. Our challenge, in the midst of the hustle and bustle of our other responsibilities, is to enjoy every moment as it is wrapped in love.

I got great help from my mum Teresa, whom I would have been lost without. She would come up daily to my house and give me a break from the children. She devoted her life to my children and taught them old Irish songs and how to dance. 7 Drunken Nights, The Little Woman from Wexford and I want to Dance with You, echoed through the House on numerous occasions! It is a beauty to behold the unbreakable bond and love that grows between a Grandparent and their grandchildren. The wisdom of their stories is TIMELESS. My mum offered unconditional love and support in both the good and bad times. Her favourite song is 'I'm on the Top of The World' by the Carpenters. We should appreciate every present moment as these moments are Heaven on earth.

Chapter Five
What is Cancer?

By this time, Benny had opened up his own business in Ardee. He was often away working long hours trying to grow his client file and upgrade the premises that he had bought. I was working part time in the bank, while spending all my free time at home trying to nurture our family. Unknown to either of us, we slowly drifted apart. Our main mistake was not talking about or expressing our feelings... WE DIDN'T KNOW HOW!!! Our marriage ended, but thankfully our friendship didn't and it continues to endure. A Huge CHOICE to make. I believe that when two people grow apart, this is part of their DESTINY. Our time together had ended on one level, however it started on another. Choosing forgiveness instead of bitterness is key. Our relationship took on a new role but with a shared purpose. As parents to our beautiful twins Ben and Leanne, we worked, and continue to work together daily to create a better future for them. Benny will always be their dad, the dad that God chose for them and I will always be their mum. Our children are our PRIDE & JOY and we are so proud of them. They are outstanding in all of their achievements. We love them both dearly.

After my marriage broke down, my energy levels were low and I felt frustrated and lost. I soon learned that how you feel on the inside attracts outer circumstances and that the external portrayal of life is a mirror image of all that is going on within. And this was definitely the case with me! I soon left my job in the bank as my Aura was scarred with grief and trauma after my marriage break up and I could not pretend to be ok. I started working part time minding young children with my sister in law, Lucy, in her Creche in Togher. This job was so rewarding. Children are like little sponges. They feel your energy. During this time, Lucy and I started using Angel Cards. Each day we would pick a card. After a while we realised that the cards were telling us the Truth. The truth was that I needed HEALING. I must admit that every romantic relationship that I had ever been in had broken down. I now realise that this was not due to outer circumstances or to the men that I met, but down to me, as my inner kingdom was insecure and powerless. It was due to my fear, my loneliness, my failure to believe in myself. I was AFRAID to move forward. I was AFRAID of change. I was AFRAID to make new choices. Inevitably, I was AFRAID of myself. This fear, this pain, these emotions became me. They grew inside of me and took over my body and my being. As a result, I got sick!

HOW DID I GET SICK?

I STOPPED LIVING!

I STOPPED SEEING!

I STOPPED FEELING!

I was ALIVE but DEAD on the INSIDE!

My FLOW HAD BEEN BLOCKED!!!!!

I STOPPED MANIFESTING

I believe that when you stop believing and manifesting your dreams into reality, you stop living. I was BLOCKED. I decided to do some Inner Journey Work, working on the physical and emotional aspects of my being. I consulted a friend of mine who practiced in this field. I arrived to her home and settled myself on her therapy bed. I needed this stagnant outdated energy to clear. The energy of abandonment, loss, betrayal, and loneliness overcame me. As I reflected on the memories of my father's death, my marriage breakup and endless broken relationships, I held deep pain in the core of my being. This pain lingered after the treatment. When your body speaks to you, do not run away. Surrender to the emotion. Accept this human frailty with all its Grace. It's asking for help. It's telling you that it's time to take action and release these broken memories.

After a few months had passed and many hospital visits, scans and tests had been carried out, I was finally diagnosed with Non-Hodgkin's Lymphoma by the medical team in Our Lady of Lourdes Hospital in Drogheda. Because I was so young, only 39 years old, and had never been sick before in my life, I got it very hard to get diagnosed. On endless occasions, I would travel to the hospital with a deep pain, to be told that there was nothing wrong with me. I was emotionally drained and physically exhausted. On this occasion however, a friend had advised me to exaggerate how I was feeling, so as I lay on the bed I screamed loudly every time the doctor touched me even if I wasn't sore. I needed medical assistance and treatment so badly.

I remember so clearly the day that the Doctor looked me in the eye and said, I know you are telling the truth. I can see it in your eyes. Relief! Someone believed me. He said 'I will do everything to help you and find out what is wrong with you'.

Non-Hodgkin's Lymphoma is a form of cancer that begins in the body's white blood cells and primarily attacks the immune system. I finally got the health care I needed and was sent for a scan. Would you believe that on the day of the scan, my dear friend, Karen, gave me a piece of cloth, a Padre Pio relic. I put this cloth in my knickers! May Padre Pio forgive me but I needed his comfort, support and healing so badly. It's amazing how the acquisition of the cloth came about. Karen had phoned me the night before to say that she had the cloth. I was leaving so early the next morning to go to the hospital that I didn't have time to meet her. But the Universe had a different idea! As we were driving through Ardee, a car pulled out in front of us, giving us a shock. Benny (yes, despite no longer being in a married relationship, our ongoing friendship meant that he would remain the person that I could depend on in my hour of need and a person who continued to accompany me on my journey) slammed on the brakes and came to a halt. He beeped the horn loudly in anger. The driver's door of the car opened and out popped Karen. She ran over waving the cloth in the air. I didn't know whether to laugh or cry. Talk about Divine Timing!

I remember being terrified as I was rolled into the large scanning machine. I was told to hold my breath and not to move so that they could get a clear picture. Tears rolled down my cheeks with the pain of trying to lie still on the table. A lovely nurse held my hand. I was wheeled back to my room and told that a doctor would be with me shortly. My children were in the room with their dad watching TV. The door opened and the doctor asked me and Benny to come with him and asked the children to remain in the room. As the doctor discussed my diagnosis, I blanked. I heard the word cancer and automatically froze. I didn't know what to expect. Was I going to be ok? Who would mind my children? How was I going to get through this on my own?

WHAT IS CANCER?

Cancer is a huge ENERGY BLOCK.

I didn't LOVE MYSELF.

I felt a FAILURE.

I felt like I was not GOoD enough.

I felt like I was ALONE and ABANDONED.

All my emotions were trapped inside me, eating away at me.

On reflection, I now realise that I was looking for love on the outside from others. I wanted someone to love and someone to love me. However, as a result I forgot how to love myself on the inside. As humans, we are unaware of the Higher Power available to us. This God Essence always on tap flows from your Soul Star, the chakra above your head like a Golden Energy Cord of Divine Love and Light into your being and clears your chakras, flowing down the meridians in your body, bringing you into full alignment with your Soul's Calling, getting you into your own Vortex. It is known as Energy. Energy is everywhere and in everything. We are ENERGY. No matter what belief system you have been brought up with, this is your Divine Birthright, always flowing. energising and clearing, releasing and letting go if you allow it to. Tapping into this Divine Consciousness is like winning the lotto. Your health is your wealth. Move your energy from your mind, through your body and into your Soul. You are a Being of Light.

I was never actually alone or abandoned, I just felt like I was. I had forgotten where I came from and the Beautiful

Soul that I AM. The I AM presence. I never ever realized how truly loved I was until the day I was admitted to hospital for chemotherapy. It felt like the hospital lit up like a space ship with all the love, blessings and prayers that were sent my way like a heart wave of love. It was only then that I realised how much love, support and care I had from multiple angles-my family, my friends, my ex-husband. My Higher Self. Everyone was rooting for me. I just needed to make a choice. I needed to decide to root for myself. I needed to decide that I would get better. I needed to decide that I would beat cancer. I needed to decide that I wanted to LIVE again and connect to my Soul's Calling., to answer the question; "Why am I here on earth"? Don't be like me and wait to be sick to WAKE UP or for life to give you a kick in the ass. I accepted the conventional therapy as well as the holistic approach as I believe they both go hand in hand.

WAKE UP NOW!

CANCER WAS MY WAKEUP CALL!

"HELLO, JENNIFER MARIA MADDY"!

Chapter Six
I am a survivor

Developing Cancer was actually a gift for me. I had deep rooted issues inside of me that needed to be brought to light, deep emotional feelings that had been buried in my body, dead emotions that were not serving me now for my highest good and highest healing. My Cancer was held in my belly, my Power Centre. I know now that I was looked after by a higher Power. The day that I was admitted to Hospital, I met a beautiful nurse named Tiny in Drogheda. She asked me; "Why are you here?" I replied; "I have Cancer". Her response changed my life. She said. "I speak to you as your Angel and you are going to be ok." Thank god I heard her words and they sank deep into my sub conscious mind. I BELIEVED HER! I BELIEVED IN MY ANGELS! This was the beginning of my self-healing journey. I have been given a second chance at life and I am so grateful to God that He has allowed me this time with my children, my family and friends. My children were only 12 years old at the time of my diagnosis. They had experienced family breakup and their mum being diagnosed with Cancer all in a very short period of time. This influenced my will to live. It was so strong. I listened to all the messages I received from loved ones and chose life and accepted my fate with faith, a huge healing in itself; Faith Healing.

ACCEPTANCE is KEY.

Another day whilst in Drogheda Hospital waiting for my results, I bumped into Father Hogan a well know priest in our community. He asked me if I was a fortune teller as I had a colorful scarf on my head covering my hair loss. I laughed and said; "Maybe you can tell me my fortune, I have Cancer". He responded by offering me the Bread of Life and a healing. His words were, "Your sins in this lifetime are forgiven, Go in Peace". Such powerful words! It was these words that allowed me to see that if you change the way you look at things, the things you look at will change. I became resilient. I became compassionate. I focused on ME!

WHO IS JENNIFER?

WHAT DOES JENNIFER WANT FOR JENNIFER?

WHAT DOES JENNIFER LIKE TO DO?

God works in mysterious ways. He gives us lessons and difficult circumstances in life to help us grow. How we accept the challenges he throws at us is our choice. We are all on a powerful journey. No one is more special than anyone else. We are all finding our path and the tools we need to navigate those paths, and although we may stumble on broken roads, our inner compass points us in the right direction every time. Life is not always perfect, but trusting the process awakens a new sense of belonging and purpose. It allows us to find ourselves; the most important person in our life. It puts us in alignment for our highest good and highest healing. By believing and having faith that we are always in the right place at the right TIME and by embracing the serendipity of life I am able to relax and to let go and let God. I allow the God Essence that flows within to flow freely through me every day.

I AM A SURVIVOR

I AM LUCKY AND I AM BLESSED

I believe that we have two choices in life, the choice to either remain a victim or to become a survivor. 9 years later, I am in awe of my life and the person that I have become. I have finally learned HOW TO EXPRESS MYSELF. I have let go of people, places and situations in my life that are not providing me with any positivity, joy or happiness. I have thanked the universe for the lessons I have been given and invited new people, places and situations into my life. I won't lie and say that this has been easy, but I have found the courage to stand on my own two feet and enjoy the things in life that are important to me, and that makes me happy. I love learning and growing. I am always watching out for signs from the Universe, and I listen. When I hear a message repeated 3 times over a short period of time, I take action to see if there is something I need to do or somewhere I need to go. It's great fun putting all the pieces of the jigsaw of life together.

My 40th Birthday Party. 6 months after my Cancer Journey.

One day, my brother Andrew saw a van driving around Dundalk, with 'It's a Sign' written on it. He sent me a photo of the van as a joke. He is always joking. Anyhow, a few days later for the first time I noticed this same van parked on the road. I had such a laugh, jumping out of my car and standing beside the van, taking a photo and sending it to Andrew, my inner child so alive. It was a sign from the Universe for sure.

I HAVE LEARNED HOW TO GRIEVE AND LET GO OF SITUATIONS OUTSIDE OF MY CONTROL, PARTICULARLY OF DEATH AND LOSS.

Death and loss are natural occurrences and we grieve so much after a loss which is only natural. If we could only realise that the souls of our departed loved ones are finally at peace and floating back happily to the light, their work here complete, their Soul Contract fulfilled, then we would celebrate their time with us and the connection we had been blessed to share. Remember, they are always with us in our memories, in our heart, giving us a heart hug whenever we need one.

After being diagonised with Cancer and having two young children to support, money became a worry. How was I going to live? I wasn't fit to work as I didn't have the energy. My mum Teresa remembered that I had a Life Assurance policy that I had been advised to take out while working in the Bank. This was my life line. I made the phone call to the Bank. They assured me not to worry as I had serious illness cover attached to this policy. What a huge relief! I sent in all my doctors' reports and waited for a cheque to be posted. It took a long time and one day, I became very emotional and begged my beautiful soul friend Linda McDonnell for help. Linda and I had job shared during my time in the Bank. Linda was an Angel. She was a pure lady and so beautiful within and without. She had previously been the Maytime Festival Queen in Dundalk. Linda had sadly passed over a few years earlier from Cancer. I had her photo on my bedside locker. "Please help me Linda," I cried. Later that evening, as I arrived in my mum's house, I checked the letter box and there was my cheque! I danced and cried as relief flooded through my body. I was over the moon. Shortly after leaving the house, my phone rang and my mum Teresa told me that a bouquet of flowers, beautiful roses had just arrived for me. There was a little note on the flowers. It was signed by Anna, Linda's mum who lived in Drogheda. My beautiful buddy and soul friend Linda had sent me a sign from Heaven. Thank you, Linda. I love you.

Never be afraid to ask your loved ones in spirit for help. They are always with you, supporting and loving you and delighted to give a helping hand. Open that channel. It's like making a phone call to Heaven. Lift that phone and believe that what's for you won't pass you, all in Divine Time. When one door closes, another door opens.

The Universe has sent many soulmates, friends and family my way to support and guide me on my journey. I won't name each and every one of you, but you know who you are. I am so grateful and I thank each and every one of you from the bottom of my HEART. I am now cancer free and I walk in the light with positivity and most importantly, with a smile. I wish everyone peace and success in their chosen field. I LOVE MY LIFE. I LOVE MYSELF. MY HEART IS OPEN. Doors have opened for me and now, at last, I am not afraid to walk through them. I have finally found my vocation, my creative expression. I am so grateful and I live in constant gratitude. Believe me, when fear comes up and I struggle, I ask God & his Archangels, angels, saints, guides and the Holy Spirit for help. I invite the Universe to help me. As I sit here in my new home after spending a peaceful day with Leanne and Ben, my new partner, our family and friends and of course our dogs, I reflect on my life and the choices I have made. I can confidently say that I have no regrets. I am Who I Am. I have also learned how to SAY NO. Duality, Light and Darkness, Yin and Yang, balance exists in my life. We constantly tend to please other people, thinking they will love and respect us if we keep trying to please them. This is so untrue. Look deeply into your body and ask, "Does this feel right?" "Does making this decision make me happy?" And take time to listen to your gut instinct, for the answer is invaluable. Be true to you. You are worthy. You deserve respect and love. By respecting yourself first, you reflect respect back to you. By loving yourself first, you reflect back love. What is reflecting back to you in your Life?

Chapter Seven
Finding my roots

In 1993, shortly after my dear dad Denis Maddy died, my mum Teresa and I were in Dublin shopping. My mum is a great character and full of fun, a beacon of love and light. She has been a great mentor in my life. As we walked around the streets of Dublin, we began to talk about my adoption. My mum decided to show me the place that I had been adopted from, Cunamh in Anne Street. I had previously worked in TSB Bank in Grafton Street, almost directly across the road! I had, unbelievably walked past this doorway on numerous occasions, not knowing the significance of it in my life! Opening this doorway and this new chapter in my life was spontaneous but the greatest leap of faith. We went in and left my details and asked if they would help me trace my birth family. I went about my life as usual, and one day out of the blue, I received a phone call from Cunamh. They had traced my birth family, the O'Sullivans from Castlemaine in Co. Kerry. What a co-incidence! I had attracted the name Sullivan through marriage! I was deeply saddened in my heart when Anne, my Counseller from Cunamh, told me that my mum Kitty O'Sullivan had passed away. I was never going to hug her and feel her arms wrapped around me. But over the years, I have been truly blessed and have received a spiritual hug from her. Kitty had passed away on our Lady's Day the 15th August, 1994.

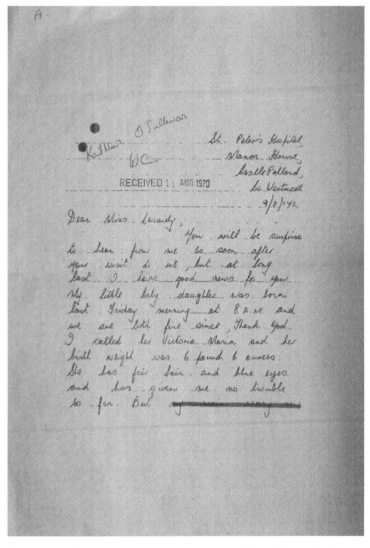

A.

Kathleen O'Sullivan
W C

RECEIVED 1 1 AUG 1970

St. Peter's Hospital,
Manor House,
Castle Pollard,
Co. Westmeath
9/8/70.

Dear Miss Cassidy,

You will be surprised
to hear from me so soon after
your visit to us, but at long
last I have good news for you.
My little baby daughter was born
last Friday morning at 8 a.m and
we are both fine since, thank God.
I called her Victoria Maria and her
birth weight was 6 pound 6 ounces.
She has fair hair and blue eyes
and has given me no trouble
so far. But ~~~~~~~~~~~~~~~~

*Finding my Roots. Letters written by my Birth Mum Kathleen
O'Sullivan, received from Cunamh, The Adoption Agency In
Anne Street, Dublin last year.*

Dear Miss Barowsky

I've just received a letter
from my mother telling me you're trying
to contact me. She said some Social worker
from Tralee has been calling on her
for quite a while now — but she didn't
want to tell me. She knew everything
about me now — after all this time —
I might as well have stayed at home.
I thought I'd signed all papers
concerning my little daughter. I'm sure
she's fine, and I have no
intention of claiming her back after
all this time. She's definitely better off
in a proper home — where she
can have all the things I can't
afford to give her, as well as
love and security.

If you still want

I was so excited at the same time to hear that my grandmother Tesse, Kitty's mum was still alive, a link connecting me to my birth family. A feeling of excitement rippled through my body, a wave of hope and light. Embarking on a new chapter in my life, I took a trip to Castlemaine a quiet country village in County Kerry when my Twins were only 3 months old. My granny was a small lady. I think she found this visit difficult as I resembled my birth mother and this triggered difficult emotions for her. She kept making tea, and leaving the room.

She gave me a beautiful gold pendant with 'Mum' engraved on it as a gift.

On a later visit to Cork, I was introduced to aunts, uncles and cousins. This bond is remarkable as our souls recognise each other. It was as if we had never been apart. We sang old Irish ballads and my granny confided that she used to use Angel Cards too when she was my age. I must have inherited this gift from her! It was here that I discovered that I have 3 half-sisters in England. We have made contact since and have started developing our relationship slowly over the past few years. I also was told that a baby boy was also given up for adoption. I put a wish out to the Universe that one day I would met him in person. When you believe, dreams do come true. Reach for the Stars with your Dreams and Desires and don't compromise.

Picture of Kathleen O Sullivan my Birth Mum.

Chapter Eight
Opening new doors

Life was very busy at home raising my children. I tried my best to keep in contact with my birth family in Ireland and England, writing and sending pictures. I was thrilled when I received an invitation to my youngest sibling, Kerry's wedding in England. My mum, Teresa, and I crossed the Irish Sea to attend the wedding. As I sat in the Church with my sisters Vicki, Fiona and Kerry and their families, listening to the songs from the choir, watching my youngest sister get married to her soulmate, it felt surreal, amazing to be part of a greater soul family cluster. We had a great time mingling and talking to everyone and getting to know them better. I overheard a conversation between my mum and my aunt Bridie. My mum, Teresa asked the question "Who is Jennifer's Dad?" This led to another door being opened which I believed was a necessary step in the journey. Sometimes in life, opening new doors can be scary. You don't know what you will find. A friend of mine advised me to visualise meeting my dad for the first time. When I took time to meditate and do this visualisation, some part of my consciousness opened up and I cried. I knew then that I was ready to embark on this new chapter of my life. I was inspired to phone my birth mum's sister Bridie in Cork to ask for help. She was delighted to assist and we made a date to go to Tralee.

The day I travelled to Tralee was one of the most amazing days of my life. I was definitely guided by my Angels. My cousins Teresa and Rosie and my aunt Bridie were more than helpful. My cousin Rosie took time out and made a map and we travelled the road to Tralee and went from door to door, knocking on each one in turn. We found nothing but loose ends for quite some time and were beginning to give up hope. At the final house on our map, we asked an old man, "Do you know the Power Family?" He replied "Yes". Fate had stepped in! My birth dad's home house was just 3 minutes away. We pulled up outside the house, a little old country cottage. My aunt Bridie walked up to the door. It was slightly ajar and she walked in. We waited in the car holding our breaths. Finally, after what felt like an eternity, the door opened and my aunt waved to me to enter. A man stood there. As I walked to the doorway, I began to wonder. Could this be him? Could this be my birth father? This man turned out to be my birth dad's brother. He embraced me and said "Your blood is my blood". We looked so alike! He told me to take a seat and he lifted the phone. After a few minutes, he handed the phone to me. I heard a man's voice on the phone. His first words were "I always hoped this day would come and all I can say is today is a beautiful day". It was him. It was my birth father!

A wise mentor and spiritual teacher of mine advised me that to be whole and balanced you must connect to both the masculine and the feminine qualities of your DNA and marry the two together. Finding both parents if possible helps this process, as you connect with your ancestors and the tree of life. If you cannot trace your family, I advise you to surrender to this emotion. Never force something to happen. If it's not meant to be, accept this fate. Energy follows Intention. Holding the thought and actively and consciously being aware of this energy and thought process is the key. Connecting telepathically soul to soul and sending love through a heart link releases this emotion with love. I must admit, I felt more alive with this new found knowledge about my roots. I finally felt more stable and balanced and my previous path in life reflected more meaningfully back to me. All the learning I had received through my previous life experience had gifted me wisdom and strength.

My birth dad's surname is POWER. This touched me as I felt that I had always had the power buried within, I had just lost sight of it through life's challenges. My cancer had been in my stomach, my power centre, which was now clear and stronger than ever. Over the following months, I sent pictures of Ben, Leanne and me to my birth dad. We took our time developing a healthy relationship. He is kind and gentle with a great sense of humour! He was a member of the Kerryblue Band and found it funny that we always had a Kerry Blue dog in my family home as a child!

What happened next on my journey was the icing on the

cake. I received a phone call from Cunamh to say that my birth brother had made contact. I was standing in my former Secondary School the day the phone call came through. An ordinary day at work was transformed. My heart missed a beat, and I felt so much JOY. I was so excited and elated. My wish had come true. Because of my previous history with social workers in Cunamh over the previous 20 years tracing my birth family, Cunamh decided to give me his phone number. That evening, I dialed his phone number and talked to my half-brother, Matt, for the first time. We had a special conversation and the closeness and bond was electric, our blood and soul connection, unmistakable. Matt currently has his own international business. His message is to 'Share the Love' through his work. This connection came to me with perfect divine timing as I was travelling to London the following week to meet my birth dad and his family in person for the first time. I told Matt this and invited him to meet up with me. It was time to 'Share Our Love'!

As the plane landed in London, I felt so nervous and excited at the same time. I was meeting my birth dad for the first time. How would I recognise him? What would we talk about? What if he didn't like me? These questions and a thousand others floated around in my head! As I walked into Arrivals, I looked about. I recognised him instantly! There, standing to meet me was my birth dad, Anthony Power! I had always prayed to Saint Anthony. He helps you find things that are lost. He had definitely helped me to find myself and my family! My birth dad was smaller in person than I had imagined. We embraced; a hug held in for a lifetime, expressed in a moment but to be cherished for an eternity. We held each other so tightly. Warmth and love flooded through my veins. Timeless Love. A precious moment shared. We started walking towards the car and we soon fell into step with each other. There was no need to be afraid, no place for fear in this moment of pure love, a moment that was divinely orchestrated. We arrived to his home and I felt so welcome. Photos of Ben, Leanne and me were on his mantlepiece, the photos that I had posted in my letters to him. I met his daughter, Katrina who has special needs. His wife Mary embraced me too. His son James wasn't there at the time as he lives in America. My heart opened like a lotus blossom in this beautiful family setting.

My birth dad drove me to a hotel to meet my brother who had also been given up for adoption within 2 years of my birth. My poor birth mum and the choices she'd had to make. We are so grateful that she chose to give us the gift of life. We walked into the hotel and waited in anticipation for my brother to arrive. Time stood still. I was overcome with nervous excitement and my mouth went dry! As he walked towards me, I remember feeling as though time had stood still, like a moment held in a parallel dimension. UNREAL, BUT SO VERY REAL!

It was like looking into a mirror, my mirror image. My birth dad witnessed this reunion and he was speechless. My brother and I looked so alike. We have the same nose! My nose is pretty unique like the lead character, Samantha's nose in Bewitched, a TV series, that I used to watch frequently as a child! Maybe I embody that energy inside of me too, as I sometimes think a thought and it usually happens in DIVINE TIMING. I think this is because I stop, look and listen to my own intuition my own inner Angelic Light force. As Matt and I chatted, my birth dad recalled that my birth mum Kitty had always told him, "you can be anything you choose to be in life". Just make that CHOICE. Nothing happens until something changes. We had thankfully absorbed this vibration into our genes. On New Years' Eve 2018, my brother sent me a song containing the lyrics, 'Hey, brother, there is an endless road to rediscover. Hey sister, know the water is sweet, but blood is thicker' (AVICII). I believe this is true for us and our new found path.

Matt and his wife Hayley and I said goodbye to my birth dad, Anthony at the hotel and travelled to meet the rest of our birth family. I introduced Matt to our 3 half-sisters and their families. My youngest sister Kerry currently lives in the family home that Kitty lived in all those years back in the heart of London. The same red velvet curtains grace the windows. Timeless. Our mum in Heaven must have been dancing with joy. A full family reunion as all of her offspring were united. Although I never got to meet my birth mum in person, as she had died at the very young age of 44, I feel her Spirit is so active and alive. She is guiding us through our journey in life. She is our Angel. She is always with us. Never stop believing that when a loved one passes to Spirit that they have not left you. They may have to leave you on the physical earth but their SOUL LIVES ON. Our Ancestors support us on our journey and are only too happy to pass down their gift of wisdom. My birth mum got her wish. All she wanted was for her baby daughter to feel SAFE AND SECURE in a home where she was loved unconditionally.

Chapter Nine

WHAT IS LOVE?

TRANSCENDENT LOVE

UNITY CONSCIOUSNESS

I believe that love is just a word, a vibration, until someone special gives it a meaning and then it grows. Love is not only made for lovers. It is also for friends and family who love each other, often more deeply than lovers. A real friend is very hard to find, difficult to leave and impossible to forget.

Love is Patient, Love is Kind

LOVE IS TIMELESS

Love in essence is the EMBODIMENT of the vibration of pure joy held in our hearts which comes in waves throughout our lives. Like the waves of the ocean, it is sometimes gentle and calm and at other times, huge and turbulent. This love flows into the chambers of our heart and into all the cells in our body creating waves of love. We have to create balance in our lives and bathe in this Love Energy, opening this portal of light, welcoming this light in and surrounding our souls' mission with love. In my opinion, taking responsibility for your own emotions and feelings changes your vibration as you learn to fully love yourself. In so doing, you create self-awareness and the recognition of how you seamlessly fit into the environment around you. Our energy flows into the air and vibrates into the Universe. What is your Energy Vibration like?

FAMILY

You do not have be blood family to be loved. People who adopt, foster or sponsor children are opening their hearts to pure unconditional love. Giving ALL children a safe SPACE is priceless. These are our soul families. A responsible person who takes on the role of parenting, sponsoring or mentoring a child is in a vocation that is undervalued in this world at this moment in time. We are all role models and mentors for ALL children. Each one of us is simultaneously both the student and the teacher. Children are watching us and our behaviours. Sometimes, as adults, we fall down at certain moments in life as difficult and challenging life events take over. More than ever in these moments, our own INNER CHILD wants to be nourished and our creativity needs to flourish again. By taking baby steps daily and creating movement in our cells we allow the LIGHT TO SHINE IN as we energise, trigger and release emotions and integrate PURE LIGHT ENERGY. Never be afraid to admit failure. When you fall, pick yourself up and in your own time, crawl, walk or run again. Climb that mountain. We need ME TIME. Put your hand up and wave your little white flag for care and attention! We must be true to ourselves and ask for help. We must be OPEN and FREE TO EXPRESS OUR EMOTIONS, BE THEY GOOD, BAD. OR INDIFFERENT and mind our own business when it comes to judging the emotions or actions of others if they are not directly affecting us. Concentrate on your own path and never mind what anyone else is doing or thinking. If the actions of others are adversely affecting us, we need to be assertive in our expression of our own needs whilst at the same time, recognising potential pain and hurt as a catalyst for their behaviour. In this way, hurts don't fester and forgiveness, and through forgiveness, healing, comes more readily. We are all learning in our own way in our own time. We can alleviate DIS-EASE and unhappy and unhelpful thoughts. We can create happy thoughts. Remember, nothing happens until something changes. Create your own Rainbow. You are the TREASURE you have always been looking for. We should not judge each other. No one is perfect. We are all perfect in our imperfections. I pray that in the future, people will come to love one another as we all have the same RED blood running through our veins. We all have the same SMILE. Planting the seeds of these new thought patterns generates the hope of CHANGE. We can nurture these new thoughts and help them flourish in Divine Time. Hopefully, there will be no differentiation between colour, race or religion, between rich or poor as we will see each other for the beautiful SOUL WITHIN and work and live together IN HARMONY for ONENESS in society

IN THE WORDS OF MICHAEL JACKSON: HEAL THIS WORLD, MAKE IT A BETTER PLACE, FOR YOU AND FOR ME AND THE ENTIRE HUMAN RACE.

Picture of myself with my Twins. Ben & Leanne.

Chapter Ten

THE FLAME OF SPIRITUAL LOVE

O Angel of God,

My Guardian Dear,

To whom God's Love, commits me here,

Ever this Day, Be at my Side,

To Light and Guard,

To Rule and Guide

Amen

Being adopted has played an important role in my life. By learning IET (Integrated Energy Therapy) healing with angels, you connect to your HIGHER SELF AND INTEGRATE the 12 Strand DNA held in our cellular memory field. Parts of my FAMILY TREE are scattered all over Ireland and England. I have traced my family and have come full CIRCLE. I have leaped off the hamster wheel. I have reconnected with my birth family and ancestry and rewritten my family history at the same time merging divine energy with the Maddy & Brennan families and extended connections. As I stated earlier, it is unbelievable that my birth mother's name was Kitty O'SULLIVAN from Kerry and I had married into my birth name! No wonder I married Benny. I was attracted to the Sullivan name!

I was given the opportunity to release my birth mum, Kitty's ashes back to the earth. By opening up to the truth of who I am, I allowed the Grace of God to shine through. My mum Kitty was cremated when she passed away. My youngest sister Kerry had held onto her ashes so tightly, never wanting to let her go. It took huge courage and strength to finally let some of her ashes go when she met me and Matt and I was privileged to be able to scatter some of her ashes when her mum Tesse passed away. I travelled to Tesse's funeral in Castlemaine in Kerry and connected mum and daughter together with the grace of our Lady. Let their spirits rest in peace forever. Amen. Also, my birth father's name is Anthony POWER from Tralee. I believe I always had the POWER. We all DO.

I now share and teach this beautiful healing therapy to clients and I am proud to be a Grand master in Reiki amongst other healing modalities. I love sharing my skills in reflexology and Indian head massage and I have mastered my own healing therapy by integrating all my skills and gifts to offer a unique service to friends, family and clients. . We all have the gift of self -healing. You are your own conduit of love and when you align your life in every area, magic takes place! Learning sacred skills to assist you on your self-healing journey reaps rich rewards. The Angels offer genuine advice and truth and are there to assist you. Their luminous light transcends and illuminates all time and space. All the unemployed

Angels are overjoyed when we ask for help! Ask, align and allow energy to flow, creating a HEARTLINK to your HIGHER POWER to help in the ascension of our planet to a higher energy platform.

I am a compassionate conduit for the Divine. It is in giving that we receive and being able to offer this facility is beyond my highest expectations. I learn daily from each student and client that I am fortunate and blessed to work with. Thank you ALL.

I also do voluntary work in Dundalk in the Cara Cancer Centre, a voluntary organisation, which has been set up to help cancer patients, their friends and family who are on this journey. They make everyone feel at home. I feel this calling is so close to my Heart. It is part of my SOUL PATH.

I sincerely thank my MUM, Teresa Maddy for believing in me and supporting me in reconnecting with my roots and navigating me through all of my life. She is my INSPIRATION and we have so much fun along the journey. Our favourite movie is Mamma Mia. My mum, son, daughter and I and our friends have watched this movie a million times!

"I HAVE A DREAM, A SONG TO SING

Picture of my mum Teresa Maddy and myself at the launch of CRYSTAL CLEAR my HOLISTIC CLINIC.

Words shared by mum Teresa Maddy

Not Flesh of my Flesh,
Not Bones of my Bones,
But still my OWN.
Never forget for one single minute,
You didn't grow under my heart,
But IN IT.

I AM NOW AT HOME WITHIN MYSELF!

"We shall not cease from exploration. And the end to all our exploring will be to arrive where we started. And know the place for the first time". T.S. ELIOT.

THERE IS NO SEPARATION

OUR SOULS RECOGNISE EACH OTHER. I THANK EACH AND EVERY ONE OF YOU FOR OPENING YOUR HEARTS & FOR SUPPORTING MY JOURNEY TO FIND MY ROOTS.

SHARE THE LOVE

In Life we need the LIGHT and the DARKNESS. It is in times of DARKNESS that we learn to APPRECIATE the LIGHT.

MANIFEST

MY GOAL FOR MY FUTURE is to be the LIGHT for OTHERS, TO SHINE SO BRIGHTLY, TO SHARE MY STORY AND TO BE THE STAR LIGHTING MY OWN WAY WITH LOVE.

GROW TO GLOW

My advice is not to struggle with disappointment.
Instead, give yourself a tap on your back and say "well
done"! Learn from the experience and move on. Grow to
glow!!!

Be proud of yourself!!!

You are a unique child of the universe.

You are home. You are that which you have been
seeking. Just relax and sit around the warmth of the fire
of your own heart.

Receiving all the knowledge and wisdom through
personal growth and living life is living life. I am in
Earth School. Recently I have travelled to Castlepollard
Mother & Baby Home in Co Meath. There is so much
being uncovered by Social Media in various places in
Ireland. We resemble the Children of Lir, a beautiful
mythical legend in Ireland. The children were turned into
swans and in time, learned how to sing their HEART-
SONG over many years. The symbol is TIMELESS.
Never ending love. UNITY. Looking up the Power
Animal, Swan resonates with my Heartsong. By
connecting to and following CRIB MATES WORLD-
WIDE I am one of a worldwide family circle. Because I
believe I am a Light Worker, I recently travelled to
Castlepollard and stood under a beautiful tree on the

grounds anchoring the energy of Peace, Love and Hope through a HEART BEAM OF LIGHT. I pray for forgiveness for our past, merging into the energy of the Now, bringing Joy to our future, thinking of the children of the future, our children, their children and so on. TIMELESS LOVE. I believe my soulsong is Whitney Houston's, 'Greatest Love of All'. Learning to love yourself is the greatest Gift of ALL.

Picture taken in Castlepollard Mother & Baby Home in Co Meath. ANCHORING THE SEEDS OF LOVE HOPE AND FORGIVENESS.

PLEASE COME & EXPERIENCE A SOUL TREATMENT

SEE YOU SOON

TRANSCENDENT LOVE

MUSIC

DISCOVER YOUR OWN RAINBOW

DISCOVER YOUR GIFTS

CRYSTAL CLEAR INTENTION

OPEN YOUR HEART

BREATHE

BELIEVE

I FORGIVE MYSELF AND I SET MYSELF FREE

FORGIVE OTHERS

ONLY LOVE IS REAL

PRAYER

COLOUR THERAPY

TOUCH

STOP AND SMELL THE ROSES

INVITE THE CONSCIOUSNESS OF THE DIVINE
INTO YOUR LIFE

MEDITATION

RELAXATION

EXCERISE

DIET

DANCE

SOCIAL INTERACTION

LISTEN TO YOUR OWN DIVINE WISDOM

NURTURE YOUR INNER CHILD

INNOCENCE

JOY

SHARE YOUR LOVE

INTIMACY

BE PASSIONATE ABOUT LIFE

FOLLOW YOUR DREAMS

IGNITE THE FIRE IN YOUR SOUL

LIVE EACH DAY AS IF IT WAS YOUR LAST

KUNDALINI

INFINITY

LIVE YOUR TRUTH

THE POWER IS WITHIN

TIME

Tick tock goes the clock,

not giving us a second to breathe.

Tick tock goes the clock,

not giving us a minute to think.

Tick tock goes the clock, not giving us an hour's rest.

Tick tock goes the clock,

not giving us time to be loved.

If time is all we have, then we should use this time
wisely.

Life is so precious and we are put on this earth for a
reason.

We may not know why, but life is full of mysteries,

so let's explore this world together,

hand in hand, with love by our side.

A FRIEND!

A Friend is like a Flower,

A Rose to be Exact.

Or maybe like a Brand New Gate

That never comes unlatched.

A Friend is like an Owl,

Both beautiful and Wise.

Or perhaps a Friend is like a Ghost

Whose Spirit never Dies.

A Friend is like a Clock that Ticks Strong.

TICK TOCK MERGING IN YOUR HEART

AND IT CONTINUES UNTIL

THE END OF TIME.

Poem dedicated by Caitlin Flynn, A pupil of St Louis Secondary School, Dundalk.

44027702R00043

Printed in Poland
by Amazon Fulfillment
Poland Sp. z o.o., Wrocław